PAT
to
GREATNESS

OLUMAYOWA OKE

PATHWAY TO GREATNESS

Copyright @ 2022 by OLUMAYOWA OKE

ISBN: 9778359669726

For More Information
Email: mmgloballc@gmail.com
+1 214-524-1774

Published By:

Content

 # Introduction

Service is the pathway to honor in the kingdom of God. You cannot go far in life unless you learn and master the art of service. All positions at the topmost top of life in every profession, are reserved for those who are willing and ready to serve God and others.

Every great man or woman in history got there on the platform of service. The only place you enter from the top is the grave; but for all other places in life, you would have to begin from the bottom, you have to serve your way up. Service is the scripturally accredited route to greatness.

As children of God, we cannot afford to undermine this covenant bridge to the top. It is through service that we qualify for the many blessings of the kingdom of God.

Here is what the scripture has to say:

If they obey and serve him, they shall spend their days
in prosperity, and their years in pleasures. Job 36:11.

As a believer, you are saved to serve. One of God's primary motivations for bringing salvation to humanity is that we would serve Him without reservation. God wants us to use all that He has blessed us with to serve Him and humanity. He expects us to lay down our financial, material, physical energy, and spiritual resources for His service.

❝Every great man or woman in history got there on the platform of service.❞

Although almost everyone aspires to be great, and lead a life of significance, not many people are committed to paying the price of service. It becomes a clear case of *"many are called, but few are chosen..."*

The fact remains, that if you truly want to get somewhere in life, you must find the path and walk the path that leads to it. In other words, you have to accept one hundred percent responsibility to do whatever it takes to arrive there. That is exactly how it works with greatness.

6

Greatness does not jump on people; it will not come to you merely because you desire it. Greatness requires intentionality, hard work, persistence, and doggedness. It is reserved only for those who qualify themselves by paying the price of service.

Amazingly, for your service to be acceptable to God, you must serve consistently, faithfully, and with the attitude of humility. A service that is offered with a wrong attitude will not only be rejected by God, but it is also neither rewarded here nor in eternity. More so, your service must be motivated by love, both for God and humanity.

> **"***You cannot go far in life unless you learn and master the art of service.***"**

If you miss the opportunity to serve, you have missed the opportunity to be great. That is the primary message of this book. As you read, may God's Spirit mount upon you, and use the thoughts, insights, and concepts shared in this book to completely transform your life.

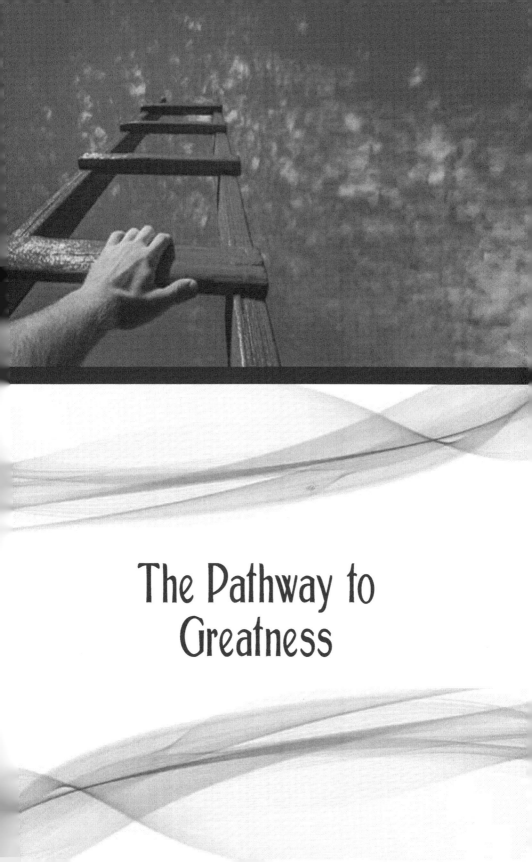

The Pathway to Greatness

C h a p t e r   O n e
The Pathway to Greatness

You are destined for greatness; created for impact and designed for the extraordinary life. Before you were born, God preordained you for a life of significance, contribution, and greatness; a life much larger, and more valuable than you can ever imagine; so, you cannot afford to remain small.

This is a very exciting yet challenging discovery to make. As believers in Christ, we have to let this truth sink deep inside of us until it becomes a major part of our consciousness.

In truth, you have no business being small, and the powerful thing is that, if you believe this truth, it will make a world of difference in every area of your existence.

Almost everyone desires to be great and influential in life, yet not everybody is willing and ready to pay the price. There is a price as well as a path to greatness — a path that leads to the topmost top in life.

Those who find that path and are diligent to walk in it always arrive at the pinnacle of life. Remember, regardless of your field of endeavor, or profession, the path to greatness is the same. It is the path of service and followership. It is true, that the possibility of greatness is available to everyone, yet not everyone will be great. Greatness doesn't jump on people.

> **"You cannot afford to remain small. God preordained you for a life of significance, contribution, and greatness; a life much larger, and more valuable than you can ever imagine."**

When it comes to greatness, you have to accept total responsibility for it, you have to decide to do whatever is required to make it your reality. Finding the path is only the beginning of the journey.

According to the Merriam-Webster Dictionary, "greatness is the quality or state of being great or enormous in skill, achievement, or power.

Greatness is the quality or state of being important, notable, or distinguished." Pathway simply means a way of achieving a specified result or a course of action. Pathway also means a series of actions that can be taken in order to achieve something. Pathway to greatness is intentionally taking a series of actions to be important, notable, and distinguished in life and destiny. The pathway to greatness is, therefore, a means by which greatness may be achieved.

Following the path of greatness is all about mapping out ways to be enormous in skill, achievement, or power, in order to leave an indelible mark in your world. In other words, to be great, you need to sit down deliberately to discover how greatness is achieved, and of course, strategize on how you can be great too. In essence, greatness is about following a well-defined path by which one may become impactful, influential, wealthy, and enormous in size.

Greatness Jumps on Nobody

Greatness does not jump on people. If you see any great man or woman in any field of endeavor, whether in politics, entertainment, sports, IT, business, or in whatever career they are in; there are things they did to get there. People become great by intentionally, and consciously making some moves, taking some steps, and doing some things in a particular way. Remember, the secrets of men are in their stories. So, you can find out people's secrets by studying them, and by learning and doing what they knew and did to be great. If you do, you too can become great.

> **"***There is a price as well as a path to greatness — a path that leads to the topmost top in life.***"**

I remember reading about a particular guy, who is a soccer superstar, called Cristiano Ronaldo. One of his former coaches, Sir Alex Ferguson, was interviewed and he said he was not surprised to see where Ronaldo had gotten in life because he knew how he evolved through paying the price.

According to him, before other players get to the field for their regular training and drills, Ronaldo would already be there, and even after others leave, he would remain on the pitch for another hour, practicing and training some more.

Also, a couple of years ago, another interview aired of one of Ronaldo's old teammates, Patrice Evra, who told the newsmen that anytime Cristiano invites you over to his home for lunch, you should eat some food before going because when you get to his house, the kind of food (mostly, vegetables and fruits) he will give you will not satisfy you.

He would tell his friends that, this is the kind of food you need to eat in order to keep fit. No wonder he is where he is today. So, greatness does not jump on people. So, in life, you are either following the pathway to greatness or running the risk of remaining permanently small. However, the good news is that once you decide and commit to following that path, greatness is almost guaranteed.

Now, the Tussle Begins

Greatness is the ultimate desire of everyone all around the world. We saw that even in the lives of the disciples of Jesus Christ. In fact, they were practically scrambling for the greatest position in what they perceived as Jesus's emerging kingdom. They were not immune to the human desire to be great. The truth is that every time, people gather together in a place, there is a tendency to power-play for greatness.

Everywhere you find more than one individual, there would be a desire to govern, lead or exercise control over others. You can call it the desire for leadership. One of the major processes that make this aspiration possible is what we call politics. So, everywhere there are human beings, there is likely going to be politics — a power play, or tussle for the government. Politics is simply the art or science of government. It refers to the activities that relate to influencing the actions and policies of a government or getting and keeping power in a government. Almost every human would want to be in charge of things and to have oversight.

> **❝People become great by intentionally, and consciously making some moves, taking some steps, and doing some things in a particular way.❞**

More so, having watched the way and manner the worldly people ruled over others like oppressors, wielding their earthly positional authority over them to their own advantage, the disciples of Jesus were influenced into desiring that kind of rulership over their fellows. It was more like a power play among them. Obviously, the power of modelling was taking a toll on them.

Let me quickly say at this point that, clearly, your model influences the direction of your pursuits. If your model is wrong, your desires will be wrong; and if your desires are wrong, your pursuits will be marred from day one. In other words, what you see will both influence your thinking and your behavior. I am sure it was wrong modeling from earthly leaders that influenced the leadership concept of the disciples of Jesus.

That explains the internal disagreement they were having over who should emerge as the greatest among them, and in response to that, Jesus delivers a keynote address to them on what we may call one of the greatest exposé on leadership and greatness:

And there was also a strife among them, which of them should be accounted the greatest.

And he said unto them, the kings of the Gentiles exercise lordship over them; and they that exercise authority upon them are called benefactors. But ye shall not be so: but he that is greatest among you, let him be as the younger; and he that is chief, as he that doth serve. For whether is greater, he that sitteth at meat, or he that serveth? Is not he that sitteth at meat? But I am among you as he that serveth. Luke 22:24-27.

Leaders Or Rulers

In the above scripture, Jesus clearly teaches that there is a

17

difference between leadership among His people from rulership in the world. Jesus was saying to them; if you want to be great, if greatness is your desire, then embrace a life of humility and service. In essence, He was saying, *"Service is the pathway to greatness"*.

Amazingly, he was not only speaking to the disciples then but also to all of us today.

> **❝Your model influences the direction of your pursuits. If your model is wrong, your desires will be wrong; and if your desires are wrong, your pursuits will be marred from day one.❞**

You know, one of the ways you know the worldly way is preeminent in a place is that those in charge "lord" things over people. In other words, they force things on the people they lead. Apparently, oppression is a worldly way of leading. You have to realize that there is a major difference between leaders and rulers. Leaders influence peoples' thoughts and actions, but rulers, rule and oppress others — forcing things down on them as their subjects.

In fact, the so-called leaders themselves are forced on the people from the onset. Usually, rulers don't ascend to greatness as legitimate leaders do.

This is why they are referred to as rulers, not leaders. For example, in African society, there are those who rule over certain localities; they are called traditional monarchs and designated as rulers or kings. One very significant thing about this group of people is that they inherited their position of rulership.

As soon as they are installed in that position, it automatically gives them oversight of everybody resident in that locality, regardless of their status. In other words, this king might even be illiterate, and has probably never been to any school; yet he would be king over all the people there, regardless of their respective degrees.

These kings are usually referred to as traditional "rulers", not traditional leaders because they are not necessarily leaders, but "rulers" who emerged purely on the basis of tribe, birth, or inheritance. Traditional rulers automatically emerge on the basis of lineage. As a result, they lord it over people, dictating what every other person should and must adhere to or do. As kings of that particular locality, they dictate the rule, meaning that whatever they say is final. That is what Jesus referred to as lording it over people.

This is totally unlike leaders who gradually become who

they are by ascending the ladder of greatness and working their way to the top. And it might interest you to know that genuine leaders are not imposed on people; instead, they grow into it, as they empower and serve others. Genuine leaders ascend into greatness through a well-defined pathway — this is what we call the pathway to greatness.

It's Written on You

It is a genuine heart of service that sets you on the pathway to greatness. I mean, genuine heart-felt service, not eye service.

You just love people genuinely, and you are serving them from your heart. In fact, you recognize great people by their service. Great people don't sit down to be served by others, instead they rise up to serve others. The rulers are the ones that sit, the leaders serve. Brian Tracy, in one of his books, 100 Absolutely Unbreakable Laws of Business Success, said something very profound. He said, *"Your rewards in life will be in direct proportion to the value of your service to others."* If your reward level is low right now in any facet of your life, check your service level.

You cannot be rewarded beyond the quality and quantity of service you render to others. In business, for example, it is the number of people you serve with your products and services that determines your income. In other words, the more people you serve with your value, the greater you will be in life. As a believer, service is one of the motivations for your salvation. In other words, you are saved to serve.

> **"Genuine leaders ascend into greatness through a well-defined pathway — this is what we call the pathway to greatness."**

Several times in the book of Exodus, God clearly instructed Moses to tell Pharaoh to let go of His people, so they could serve Him.

> *And thou shalt say unto him, The Lord God of the Hebrews hath sent me unto thee, saying, let my people go, that they may serve me in the wilderness...*
>
> *Exodus 7:16.*

In the New Testament, the Scripture also shows us that once we are saved, we are to serve God. God did not save us to serve our interests and agenda, but to serve His interests and His agenda.

> *That he would grant unto us, that we being delivered out of the hand of our enemies might serve him without fear. Luke 1:74.*

You Are Helping Yourself

Service is a divine imperative for everyone given the privilege of the new life in Christ, and beyond that for everyone who desires to be great in life.

Here is a statement made by Ralph Waldo Emerson: *"It is one of the most beautiful compensations of life that no man can sincerely try to help another without helping himself."* When you're helping people, you are invariably helping yourself without knowing. In other words, you are already on the path to greatness.

Do you know that whenever you give to some people, it looks as if those people are using you, but in the real sense, you are the ones using them? Remember, the scripture says,

   "it is more blessed to give than to receive." (Acts 20:34).

In essence, no one can successfully use you. Whenever there is an opportunity for you to give, realize it's your opportunity. Never be a parasite leeching unto people with the intention of using them, rather be of service to them.

Nothing Goes for Free

As a person geared towards greatness, you must be wary of free things. Most free things have a lot of strings attached. In other words, a lot is lost without you actually knowing. For example, some young ladies engage in something popularly called, "aristo" or "runs" in some parts of Africa.

You see a younger girl in her twenties or maybe early thirties, who goes around having sexual relationships with older men, in their fifties, sixties, or even seventies for monetary benefits. I am talking about men old enough to be their fathers or grandfathers. In return, these men give these ladies huge sums of money, most times, in hard currencies.

> **"**Service is a divine imperative for everyone given the privilege of the new life in Christ, and beyond that for everyone who desires to be great in life.**"**

Sometimes these ladies think that they have used the men since it took only a few hours of interaction for which they receive heavy financial returns.

Unfortunately, what these ladies fail to realize, is that they are the ones really being used by these men. If these ladies know what they have taken away from their bodies in exchange for money, they will fall face-down and weep.

Or why would someone be willing to part with upward of $10,000 just to have fun with a girl for one night? Of course, he must be after something more valuable than you can even begin to imagine. You think about it.

You might not believe it, but if you get involved with such people, they will use your destiny, and your glory to renew their powers in the occultic groups. That is how many of the men continue to rise in politics, business, and in all kinds of funny things they do. In fact, everything the girls are supposed to use to prosper is taken from them.

When these young ladies think they are using those men, they should realize that they are the ones actually being used. Beware of trying to get something for nothing. It is a dangerous route to follow. Instead, choose to follow the art of giving and service.

The truth is, when you are serving, you may think you are the least, but Jesus actually said, you are the greatest. So, when it looks like you are a fool because you are serving others, realize that you are on your way to greatness. Remember what Ralph Waldo Emerson said, "serve and thou shalt be served."

Barack Obama

Again, genuine heart-felt service is what sets you on the path to greatness. Greatness is for servants, not for the bosses and rulers. A person sitting down doing nothing can never taste greatness forever. Service is how every great man or woman managed to ascend the ladder of greatness.

In fact, the act of service was how Barack Obama; emerged as the first black (African American) president of the most powerful nation on earth — the United States of America. This was in spite of his being a "person of color" or everything else that was against him, as an African American. I encourage you to find and read his biography or watch some videos on him.

You will find out that he started from community service. Barack Obama became relevant and visibly known for his impact on serving other people, especially in the southern side of Chicago. He was involved in organizing community outreaches, food drives, helping the poor, sending people to school, and pursuing other causes that were directly beneficial to others. That was where he started from, and found his way to the White House to become one of the most influential persons in the world, despite his color.

Since all great men in history, including Jesus, ascended the ladder of greatness through service, then service is clearly how you and I must ascend into greatness. Remember what Jesus said: A servant is not greater than his master. When service is perfected, mastery is achieved. This means that, when the servant is perfect, he is like his master. You cannot beat this divinely established system of lifting. In fact, this is how the master Himself (Jesus) puts it:

> *The disciple is not above his master, nor the servant above his lord. It is enough for the disciple that he be as his master, and the servant as his lord.*
>
> *Matthew 10:24-25.*

Serving others is not a disadvantage, instead, it is an advantage. Serving others is the greatest thing you can do for yourself, and your future.

The question, therefore, is this; are you truly proactively engaged in serving God and others?

Do you genuinely serve from your heart?

Do you value service as the God-ordained pathway into greatness? Have you decided to follow the path of greatness? If you understand and embrace this truth, then you are definitely on your way to greatness. Remember, only genuine servants taste greatness.

I pray for you that as you accept a hundred percent responsibility to pay the price of greatness and get involved with serving God, and others, your greatness shall know no bound in the name of Jesus.

I pray that your name will become a household name in your chosen field, career, or business. You will not be lost in the crowd. The power of the Holy Ghost will distinguish you, and you will not be small!

Aspects of
Service

Chapter Two
Aspects of Service

There are many ways by which we may offer acceptable services to God. Without understanding these indices, the concept of offering service to God will remain completely absurd.

There have to be some clear parameters by which service may be adequately measured. Otherwise, you won't be able to ascertain whether you are truly serving God or not. I must emphasize that it is important to serve God acceptably. You have to serve God the way He wants you to serve Him, not necessarily the way you want to do it. The scripture speaks about having the grace to serve God acceptably:

Wherefore we receiving a kingdom which cannot be

moved, let us have grace, whereby we may serve God acceptably with reverence and godly fear. Hebrews 12:28. You can serve God in a way that is acceptable to Him. It is also possible to serve in a way that is not acceptable to Him. We will focus on spiritual service to God in this chapter, and in the next chapter, we would examine another possible way to serve God.

Spiritual Service

Offering God spiritual service is the first and most important aspect of service to God. Every other avenue of service to God finds impetus from our spiritual service to Him. Spiritual service is, however, divided into many parts, some of which will be explained in this chapter. It is pertinent to say that no matter the kind of spiritual service we desire to offer to God, the most important is 'Worship.' The Book of **John 4:23-24** explains the major reason for this stance:

> *But the hour cometh, and now is, when the true worshippers shall worship the Father in spirit and in truth: for the Father seeketh such to worship him. God is a Spirit: and they that worship him must worship him in spirit and in truth.*

Jesus made it clear how much the Father seeks for those that will worship Him in spirit and in truth at all times.

Emphasis on 'seek' which is a word that expresses the desire of God to find people who will dedicate themselves to Him in the area of worship as He cannot worship Himself. However, in this chapter, the focus will be on spiritual service in three other major areas that are also extremely important in our service to God as believers.

> **" Offering God spiritual service is the first and most important aspect of service to God. "**

I): Prayers for the Expansion of God's Kingdom on Earth

The first way to render spiritual service unto God, beyond worshipping Him, is to prioritize prayers for His kingdom. In Saint Luke's gospel, the Bible reveals the order and focus of a believer's prayer life in what we usually refer to as the Lord's prayer. Jesus' disciples came to Him requesting that He teach them how to pray.

Having watched with amazement, the ease with which Jesus commanded the supernatural, with tangible and undeniable results that followed His ministry; and knowing that prayer was the secret behind such results, they came and asked Jesus to let them in on the subject of prayer. They had probably been praying without positive results, so they wanted to know what made Jesus' prayer produce results consistent whereas theirs wasn't producing.

> *And it came to pass, that, as he was praying in a certain place, when he ceased, one of his disciples said unto him, Lord, teach us to pray, as John also taught his disciples. And he said unto them, when ye pray, say, Our Father which art in heaven, hallowed be thy name.*
>
> *Thy kingdom come. Thy will be done, as in heaven, so in earth. Give us day by day our daily bread. And forgive us our sins; for we also forgive every one that is indebted to us. And lead us not into temptation but deliver us from evil. Luke 11:1-5.*

Although they had been praying, they were praying amiss. They were praying without following the right order and template from God. One thing is that God's things must be done God's way in order to get the right results. You have to understand God's system of doing things before you can succeed in it. For instance, if you study Matthew's account, it says:

> *Be not ye, therefore, like unto them: for your Father knoweth what things ye have need of before ye ask him. After this manner, therefore, pray ye: Our Father which art in heaven, Hallowed be thy name. Thy*

kingdom come. Thy will be done in earth, as it is in heaven. Give us this day our daily bread.

Matthew 6:8-11.

So, it says, your father knows what you need before you ask him. He knows you need healing from that sickness, you need a husband, you need children, you need a business breakthrough, you need to pass that exam, you need a good home, and so on; yet He expects you to follow the right protocol first, by praying for the kingdom.

"*God's things must be done God's way in order to get the right results. You have to understand God's system of doing things before you can succeed in it.*"

He said your father already knows that you need all those things, but you need to follow the protocol of prayers — first, it says hallowed be thy name, then next is "...THY KINGDOM come." Jesus was saying to them, don't pray for bread and butter yet, until you have worshipped God, and prayed for His kingdom.

This is called the principle of kingdom priority. Jesus was emphasizing to the disciples the missing link in their prayer life, which is putting God and His kingdom first, before their own needs. This is not to say that there is something wrong with you asking for your own need, it just has to come after you have prayed for the kingdom of God.

You cannot approach a king and go straight into making requests without first worshiping the king. It is the same thing in the natural world. A wise woman knows that once she satisfies the needs of her husband, she has his almost undiluted and undivided attention for that duration and vice versa.

Every human being will likely reciprocate and give attention to anyone that puts their needs ahead of other things. Therefore, praying for needs, though legitimate, must not come ahead of God's glory and His kingdom. That would be like doing the right thing at the wrong time. This is why the request for daily bread comes only after kingdom advancement prayers.

When you get to the prayer room, suspend praying for your needs till you have prayed for the kingdom of God. In other words, prioritize the kingdom of God in your prayers. His kingdom must come first before you mention any other thing.

The truth is, when you are praying for yourself, you are

only receiving, but when you are praying for the kingdom and for others, you are giving.

> **"*Praying for needs, though legitimate, must not come ahead of God's glory and His kingdom.*"**

The Bible makes it clear: it is more blessed than to receive. *I have shewed you all things, how that so laboring ye ought to support the weak, and to remember the words of the Lord Jesus, how he said, it is more blessed to give than to receive. Acts 20:35.*

The blessing is actually in the giving, not in the receiving. Anytime you get on your prayer altar, put His kingdom first.

II): Prayers for Fresh Oil for Your Pastors and Ministers

Another way to engage in spiritual service to God is to pray for fresh oil for your pastors, and ministers, especially the set man of your church.

Praying for the set man is something that directly impacts the lives of all the church members. If anything goes wrong with the set man, it will affect everybody under his leadership. It's just like being on a plane flight. As long as you are on board, your life is affected by the decision of the pilot.

The set man is the pilot in that spiritual organization. One way you show you care about getting to your destination and landing safely is to pray for the pilot (the set man).

Everyone on board is in danger of a crash. Pastors need fresh oil to function effectively and continue to be a blessing to the people. Otherwise, they will get worn out and become ineffective.

> *But my horn shalt thou exalt like the horn of a unicorn:*
> *I shall be anointed with fresh oil. Psalm 92:10.*

A lot of well-meaning Christians don't realize the need to pray for their pastors and ministers. Instead, they see them as superstars who do not need a form of spiritual assistance from anyone.

Could it be that the pastors themselves have sold an image of a superstar? Well, that was not the case with Apostle Paul. As anointed as he was, he constantly requested prayers from his congregants, unlike the superstar pastors and ministers of today. In the book of Thessalonians, Paul openly asked the people to pray for him along with his ministry team:

Finally, brethren, pray for us, that the word of the Lord may have free course, and be glorified, even as it is with you: And that we may be delivered from unreasonable and wicked men: for all men have not faith. 2 Thessalonians 3:1-2.

In the above scripture, he said to pray that the word of God committed to them would have a free course and be glorified. There is a need for the word of God to prosper freely in their hands and produce desired results.

"*The set man is the pilot in that spiritual organization. One way you show you care about getting to your destination and landing safely is to pray for the pilot.*"

You must pray for your pastors that they speak the word of God with boldness, audacity, and with confidence. That means, without being scared of your face or how you will respond to the word of God they are bringing to you. Some pastors do not have the boldness to teach the word of God as it is because they are afraid of how members will respond. God told Jeremiah not to be intimidated by people's faces.

If you have not pastored, you will not understand what I am talking about, because if you lead people in a pastoral and ministerial capacity, you will discover that a lot of people are specifically sent by the devil, not only to disrupt the move of God but to attack the pastors. There is usually no reason for their wickedness.

No wonder they are also called unreasonable because their evil intentions and actions just don't make sense. There are wicked and unreasonable men in every church and, most importantly, outside the church who make the pastor their target. Like the Bible rightly said, "strike the shepherded and the sheep will scatter..." When you see a shepherd or his family attacked by wicked and unreasonable men, just know that the real target is actually the sheep.

In our ministry, for example, we pray first for the church (God's Kingdom), the pastor, before praying for ourselves. We got that pattern from the Bible, and if you want to see unusual results, then you must endeavor to follow the unusual pattern.

There is order in heaven. Heaven does not respond to your tears, but to your alignment with the principles of God. Also, aside from praying for your pastor and his family, you have to look out for them.

III): Winning of Souls into God's Kingdom

The third aspect of spiritual service is soul winning. It is by far one of the greatest services you and I can render to God and His kingdom. Soul winning is extremely important to God because He sent His Son, Jesus, to die for the sake of souls.

> **"When you see a shepherd or his family attacked by wicked and unreasonable men, just know that the real target is actually the sheep."**

In reality, the greatest miracle is not a green card, a brand-new SUV, a huge amount of money in your bank account, or any material acquisition. It is not a high-paying job, a beautiful spouse, or a trip to Hawaii; thank God for all those beautiful things, and you should have them, but the greatest miracle is the miracle of salvation.

In Luke's gospel, the Bible tells us about the joy in heaven steered up by soul winning.

> *I say unto you, that likewise, joy shall be in heaven over one sinner that repenteth, more than over ninety and nine just persons, which need no repentance.*
>
> *Luke 15:7.*

Notice: It didn't say there is joy over somebody that bought a house, or that got a green card, but over one sinner that repents. So, the moment somebody says that salvation prayer, joy breaks out in heaven.

In Matthew 16:26, the Bible values one soul over every other thing:

> *For what is a man profited, if he shall gain the whole world, and lose his own soul? or what shall a man give in exchange for his soul? Matthew 16:26.*

Also in John's gospel, Jesus said that you and I should lift our eyes and look at the field because they are ready for harvest.

> *Jesus saith unto them, my meat is to do the will of him that sent me and to finish his work. Say not ye, there are yet four months, and then cometh harvest? behold, I say unto you, lift your eyes, and look on the fields; for they are white already to harvest. And he that reapeth receiveth wages, and gathereth fruit unto life eternal: that both he that soweth and he that reapeth may rejoice together. John 4:34-36.*

In other words, there are so many people that need Jesus in your neighborhood, on your streets, at your job, at your shop; I mean, everywhere around you. As you get busy winning them to the Lord, you will be rewarded by God. By the way, soul-winning is not just for pastors, it is for every child of God. God is counting on you to bring the lost into His kingdom. The book of Jeremiah describes us as God's battle-axe *(Jeremiah 51:20-22)*.

God is relying on you and me to overturn the evil systems of this world, drive away from the darkness, and shake systems, and structures everywhere for the Lord. We will not fail Him. God is calling every one of us into the business of soul-winning. Remember, like the scriptures say, that he that reapeth, receiveth wages.

When you win people to the Lord, don't just cut them loose, instead ensure they remain. Satan would want to drag people back by all means, but you must strive to ensure they remain. Jesus prayed passionately that God will keep everyone He had given to him. John tells us that we are to bear fruits and ensure they remain. There is no reward for souls that don't remain in the fold.

Ye have not chosen me, but I have chosen you, and ordained you, that ye should go and bring forth fruit, and that your fruit should remain that whatsoever ye shall ask of the Father in my name, he may give it to you. John 15:16.

When the souls you have won to Christ remain, then you

are rewarded by heaven. One of the most powerful rewards of soul winning is that your prayers will be answered. Your prayers will get answered, and your life will become a practical testament of answered prayer!

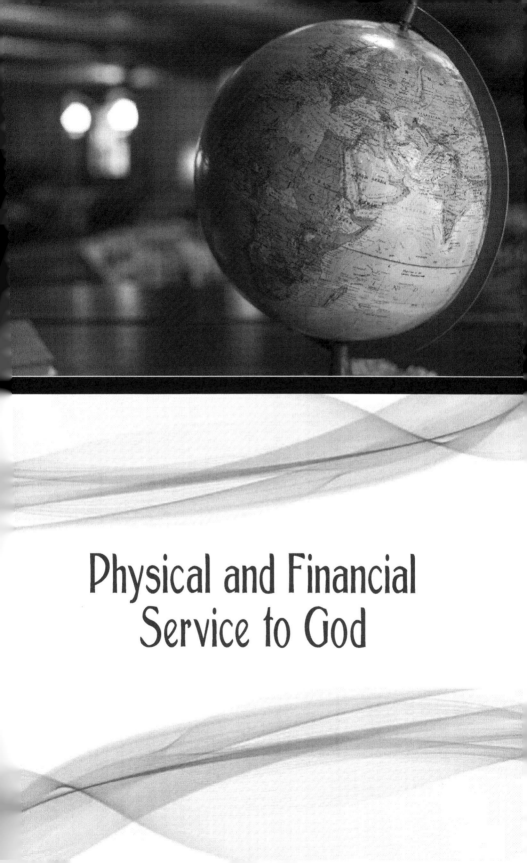

Physical and Financial
Service to God

Chapter Three
Physical and Financial Service to God

S erving God is not limited to offering spiritual service to Him, but it also involves physical things, both physical effort and financial resources.

That is the focus of this chapter. However, I will warn you ahead that before you present any physical thing or finances to God that will be accepted by Him, you must first offer yourself to the Lord as a living sacrifice, holy and acceptable before Him *(Romans 12:1).*

Before the people gave their finances to the Lord, they first gave themselves to the lord.

And this they did, not as we hoped, but first gave their own selves to the Lord, and unto us by the will of God.

2 Corinthians 8:5.

Remember, God had respect for Abel before responding positively to his sacrifice. If Abel was not first accepted by God, his sacrifice would have been a source of offense to God.

And in process of time, it came to pass, that Cain brought of the fruit of the ground an offering unto the Lord. And Abel, he also brought of the firstlings of his flock and of the fat thereof. And the Lord had respect unto Abel and to his offering: But unto Cain and to his offering, he had not respected. And Cain was very wroth, and his countenance fell. Genesis 4:3-5

.

One of the reasons why Cain's sacrifice was not accepted apart from the fact that it was not a first, or blood sacrifice, was because his person was not first accepted by God, like his brother Abel. So apart from the fact that he violated a divine order, his person was not acceptable to God. In essence, to offer God anything else, you must begin with the offering of your greatest resource — YOU! It is you first, then your physical service, or your money and any other thing.

Physical Service
Offering physical service to God involves using your

energy, talents, and skills to serve God. It is the physical expression or outworking of your spiritual devotion to God. It's all about the practicality of service to God. It is condescending from whatever status you are to get your hands dirty for the course of the kingdom of God.

For whether is greater, he that sitteth at meat, or he that serveth? Is not he that sitteth at meat? But I am among you as he that serveth. Luke 22:27.

Physical service is contributing your own quota towards the advancement of God's kingdom here on earth. It is playing your own role, laboring to see God's kingdom make substantial progress.

"To offer God anything else, you must begin with the offering of your greatest resource - YOU! It is you first, then your physical service, or your money and any other thing."

When the apostles of Jesus, leaders of the early church faced a situation where certain widows were neglected in the daily distribution, they decided to engage in division of labor, committing that aspect of ministry to a group of men who made themselves available for kingdom service.

This is seen in the scripture below:

Then the twelve called the multitude of the disciples unto them, and said, It is not the reason that we should leave the word of God, and serve tables.

Wherefore, brethren, look ye out among you seven men of honest report, full of the Holy Ghost and wisdom, whom we may appoint over this business. But we will give ourselves continually to prayer, and to the ministry of the word. And the saying pleased the whole multitude: and they chose Stephen, a man full of faith and of the Holy Ghost, and Philip, and Prochorus, and Nicanor, and Timon, and Parmenas, and Nicolas a proselyte of Antioch: Whom they set before the apostles: and when they had prayed, they laid their hands on them. Acts 6:2-3.

You know what, after they had set up this structure of service, choosing seven trust-worthy men among them to serve in an administrative capacity, the result was completely amazing. They experienced a massive increase in the word of God, resulting in significant church growth.

And the word of God increased, and the number of the disciples multiplied in Jerusalem greatly, and a great company of the priests were obedient to the faith.

Acts 6:7.

As seen in the scripture above, a great number of people, priests (religious), and influential leaders became obedient to the Faith.

> **❝***Physical service is contributing your own quota towards the advancement of God's kingdom here on earth.***❞**

Financial Service

Financial service is the third aspect of service to God. Offering financial service simply means using your money to serve God. You can either serve God with your money and financial assets, or you can serve Him without them. To serve God without your resources is not to serve Him at all, because that means, you have made your resources (your money and other assets) your god.

> *No man can serve two masters: for either he will hate the one and love the other; or else he will hold to the one and despise the other. Ye cannot serve God and mammon. Matthew 6:24.*

Jesus rightly said that you cannot serve God and mammon. However, as I said earlier, you can use your mammon (money) to serve God. Money is a very important tool for the spread of the gospel.

The book of Zechariah says that God's kingdom spreads through prosperity *(Zechariah 1:17)*.

You won't realize how powerful money is in the spread of the gospel till you see the havoc that can be done against the gospel by those who have means but hate the kingdom of God. In fact, the resurrection of Jesus was literally covered up because of money, as the soldiers who witnessed His resurrection were paid to lie and cover it up.

Money is so important in the affairs of life and the workings of the kingdom of God that you cannot serve Him without your money as a believer. Instead, you are to mobilize and make available as many resources as you can possibly lay your hands on for the furtherance of the gospel of Christ, from where you are to the ends of the earth. You must make your money available for the gospel.

Any money you cannot use to serve God is an idol. If you can't serve God with your money, it means you are serving money. Money is not meant to be served, instead, it is meant to be a tool to serve God. Unfortunately for a lot of God's people today, money has become their god.

One of the primary essences of money is worship. True worship is a sacrifice of resources at God's feet, beginning with offering the greatest sacrifice of all — your very self. Satan can allow you to worship all you can as long as you will not worship God with your means.

In Egypt, remember, Pharaoh agreed to let them go for a while to worship, but he said they should leave their resources behind, but Moses refused because the heart of true worship is sacrifice. What you literally offer on the altar of God, is true worship. One of the major essence of liberating the people of Israel from Egypt (which was a type of salvation) was worship. That was why Moses, being a very smart guy, refused Pharaoh's deal. Moses knew that worship is incomplete without money on the altar of worship, and so he refused to go without their resource.

> *And Pharaoh called unto Moses, and said, go ye, serve*
> *the Lord; only let your flocks and your herds stay: let*
> *your little ones also go with you. And Moses said, thou*
> *must give us also sacrifices and burnt offerings, that*
> *we may sacrifice unto the Lord our God. Our cattle*
> *also shall go with us; there shall not a hoof be left*

behind; for thereof must we take to serve the Lord our God, and we know not with what we must serve the Lord until we come thither. Exodus 10:24 -26.

In fact, we are told that God later gave them a strategy to take from their Egyptian masters, something that was only possible through the supernatural power of God.

God gave them such favor that they were able to eventually go away with all their master's gold and other valuables. The scriptures reveal that they literally spoiled the Egyptians *(Exodus 12:36)*.

❝True worship is a sacrifice of resources at God's feet, beginning with offering the greatest sacrifice of all — your very self.❞

Another example of someone who used his resources to serve God's agenda was the man, Cyrus. Cyrus was a heathen king that got inspired and empowered (anointed) by God to serve Him with his resources.

In fact, he provided resources for the building of God's temple *(Isaiah 45:1-3)*.

If you serve God without your resources, your service is not complete. How can you claim to be serving God without putting in your money? It's impossible!

What kind of service or empty worship is that? I know this doesn't sound politically correct, going by the new wave of social media criticism against giving; but guess what, worshipping God with your money is the scriptural pattern to follow.

The beautiful thing about using your money to serve God is that it will always come back to you pressed down, shaken together, and running over *(Luke 6:38)*. In fact,

Jesus promised that you will be rewarded for every sacrifice you make for the gospel both in this life and in the life to come. This is inclusive of your financial sacrifices to the Lord.

And everyone that hath forsaken houses, or brethren, or sisters, or father, or mother, or wife, or children, or lands, for my name's sake, shall receive a hundredfold and shall inherit everlasting life. Matthew 19:29.

Jesus talked about hundredfold returns on all our kingdom investments. In other words, you can't beat God's giving once you plant the seed (your worship, sacrifices, and service) unto God.

A good example of reaping a mighty harvest was in the case of Isaac while he was in the middle of a grievous famine *(Genesis 26:12-14)*.

This is a very powerful concept and mystery of the kingdom of God. If you catch it, it will change everything for you. Indeed, service is the true pathway to greatness. A heartfelt service to God, His kingdom, and people is the God-ordained pathway to greatness.

Moreover, even when you have attained greatness, endeavor to keep serving in all capacities. What took you up is exactly what you need to stay up. Never allow your new position or status in life to rob you of the privilege to continue to serve your master. Examples abound of those who served or still serving God despite their enviable status, some of which are briefly examined below:

King David, 'the Usher'

David, though a king of Israel, preferred to be an usher in God's house *(Psalm 84:10)*. He was a king in his palace, but

a doorkeeper in God's house. The king doubles as a doorkeeper. What a paradox! Imagine a king or president who opens the door for other people to go into the house of God. That is only possible through a heart of humility and a deep-seated revelation of service. No wonder, his greatness knows no bound.

John D. Rockefeller

John D. Rockefeller is the first American billionaire in history. He was the first person to ever make a billion dollars in the history of America. However, do you know what, he was also an usher in the church? A billionaire opening doors for ordinary people making 3 dollars an hour. That is the spirit of greatness.

Folorunsho Alakija

The richest black woman, a Nigerian by the name, Folorunsho Alakija, goes out regularly into the street for evangelism. She did not hire someone with her money to help her preach the gospel, but she literally goes out there to do it herself.

Cosmas Maduka

Another very wealthy Nigerian, Cosmas Maduka, goes out also to preach the gospel on the streets. He would usually ride his power bike to grab attention, and then once he secures the attention of his audience, he would begin to preach the gospel, serving his master. We are talking about a billionaire in dollars.

President Jimmy Carter

Do you remember President Jimmy Carter, one of America's former presidents? He lives in Atlanta, Georgia. Not too long ago, he had cancer and had to go through brain surgery. While he was still recovering, he was interviewed by CNN. The interviewer asked him, Sir, you've been home for about three months, recovering and all of that. In these three months, what did you miss doing the most? He said I miss teaching my Sunday school class in the church.

At first, I thought I didn't hear him well, but that was exactly what he said. I was totally amazed. I mean, a former American President still committed to teaching Sunday school in his church, wow!

How many people who are financially comfortable still do that in the church these days? Let alone after serving as the President of one of the most influential nations on the planet. Come on! Some people have not even achieved anything, yet they are too proud to serve God. What a shame! That also explains why many people die small, while a former president couldn't wait to return to his duty post of teaching Sunday school.

Although these people are rich, famous, and highly placed in society, they did not allow their status to rob them of their kingdom heritage of service. For everyone still on the way up the ladder of life, I want you to know beyond a shadow of a doubt that service is still the key. If you find and stick to it, I tell you, the topmost top of greatness shall be your next destination. You will not die small!

Serving God with Humility

Chapter Four
Serving God with Humility

Serving God meaningfully and acceptably requires that you serve Him on His own terms. To truly offer God service that is accepted by Him, you must do it with the right heart and attitude. Serving God without the right heart and attitude is tantamount to a complete waste of time.

If you have walked with God for a while as a believer, you would have already discovered that it is not everything offered to God that He accepts. In the previous chapter, we saw that God accepted the sacrifice of Abel, which was the expression of his service and devotion to God. However, God rejected Cain's sacrifice *(Genesis 4:5).*

In the second book of Chronicles, it was said of King Amaziah that though he served God; he did it with a wrong attitude or heart:

Amaziah was twenty and five years old when he began to reign, and he reigned twenty and nine years in Jerusalem. And his mother's name was Jehoaddan of Jerusalem. And he did that which was right in the sight of the Lord, but not with a perfect heart. 2 Chronicles 25:2.

Even though it was reported of him to have done what was right in the sight of God, the fact that he did it without a perfect heart, made it valueless before God.

❝Serving God without the right heart and attitude is tantamount to a complete waste of time.❞

Humility is Key

When it comes to offering something to God, the heart with which you do it is just as important as what you offer to Him. So, you can do something good, but if the heart is not right, you will have no reward from God. Even though you may have paid a costly price for it, it could still be a waste of time. Therefore, the heart is something to pay keen attention to. The Bible talks about the wickedness of the heart:

> *The heart is deceitful above all things, and desperately*
> *wicked: who can know it? I, the Lord search the heart,*
> *I try the reins, even to give every man according to his*
> *ways, and according to the fruit of his doings.*
>
> *Jeremiah 17:9-19.*

The heart is that part of the human being that you can't really fully understand. It is either an asset or a liability. When it comes down to the issue of offering acceptable service to God, you need a heart of humility.

Another word that we can use interchangeably with humility is the word meekness. Sincerely, you can't be humble and not serve God in His house, and you cannot serve acceptably in the House of God without being humble. It is impossible! Whenever you see humility, you will see service. Both are two inseparable twins.

What is Humility?

What's does it really mean to be humble, and what do the scriptures say about humility and service? Humility is simply the quality or state of not thinking you are better than other people: the quality or state of being humble or meek. The opposite of humility is pride. Pride is a feeling that you respect yourself and deserve to be respected by other people, it is also a feeling that you are more important or better than other people.

Pride Dethrones

Pride is the first guarantee for a fall. It does not matter the height you are in right now, the moment you allow pride to enter your heart, there is no telling how your fall will be, but falling, is guaranteed. It was pride that caused a one-time prestigious angel of heaven, Lucifer, to fall from his exalted position as the covering Cherub. Although he was originally made, through pride, he became self-deluded and corrupt, and the result was a massive fall.

> **"When it comes down to the issue of offering acceptable service to God, you need a heart of humility."**

Though he was a fascinating creature of God, who shared in intimate secrets of heaven, he desired to rule like the most-high. He became exalted in his mind, leading to his fall. The prophet Isaiah provides us with a clue as to what was responsible for the irreversible fall of Lucifer.

How art thou fallen from heaven, O Lucifer, son of the morning! How art thou cut down to the ground, which didst weakens the nations! For thou hast said in thine heart, I will ascend into heaven, I will exalt my throne

above the stars of God: I will sit also upon the mount of

the congregation, in the sides of the north: I will ascend

above the heights of the clouds; I will be like the most

high. Yet thou shalt be brought down to hell, to the sides

of the pit. Isaiah 14:12-15.

Lucifer wanted to ascend to the same spiritual pedestal as his creator. He over-estimated himself, comparing himself with God, the Most high. Pride is a killer of destiny, but with humility, you can literally ascend to the highest position available in the kingdom of God.

As a matter of fact, the kingdom of God rates humility as the highest virtue to cultivate in other to rise. However, by being proud like Lucifer, you are recruited into his army, and this will ultimately lead to your fall.

Canst, thou draw out leviathan with a hook? or his

tongue with a cord which thou lettest down?... Sharp

stones are under him: he spreadeth sharp pointed things

upon the mire. He maketh the deep to boil like a pot: he

maketh the sea like a pot of ointment. He maketh a

path to shine after him; one would think the deep to be

hoary. Upon earth, there is not his like, who is made

without fear. He beholdeth all high things: he is a king

over all the children of pride. Job 41:1, 30–34.

I deliberately started from verse one to help you understand whom the Bible is talking about in the scripture above. Leviathan, Belzebulb, and Satan or the devil are all referring to one and the same thing. See that last part, "...he is a king over all the children of pride." In other words, once you become prideful, you are ignorantly recruited into the clan of Satan. You have been recruited to join his army.

> **"The kingdom of God rates humility as the highest virtue to cultivate in other to rise."**

The Bible clearly says that the things that are written in the scriptures are written for our admonition, so that we don't become victims of Satan's trap, falling into the same error as Lucifer.

> *Now all these things happened unto them for examples: and they are written for our admonition, upon whom the ends of the world are come. 1 Corinthians 10:11.*

Look at King Saul; as long as the King was humble, he was on the throne; but as soon as his position entered his heart and he became proud, he was dethroned. Remember, it was this same king Saul who kept hiding himself the day that Prophet Samuel wanted to anoint him, as king. In fact, the Bible later said about him that he was small in his eyes.

And Samuel said, when thou wast little in thine own

sight, wast thou not made the head of the tribes of

Israel, and the Lord anointed thee king over Israel?

1 Samuel 15:17.

Saul initially had a heart of humility, but then as soon as he ascended the position of leadership as the king of Israel, began to wield the rod of authority, and enjoy the power that went with his new position, he became prideful, and eventually lost the position. It was not Samuel who determined how long King Saul reigned, it was his pride. His pride robbed him of the opportunity to continue to impact his generation.

Like in the days of King Saul, pride is still destroying and robbing countless men and women these days of their destiny of enthronement and the overall opportunity to make an impact, shape culture, and transform a generation.

Pride is a Killer

Again, I say, pride is a killer. It will kill your possibility of rising to higher heights in God. God cannot stand the sin of pride. Oh yes, God does not want us to lie, fornicate, gossip, hate, steal, or walk-in unforgiveness, these are all terrible spiritual conditions; but when it comes to pride, God hates it. Although a proud person may be an enemy of Satan, he is definitely an enemy of God. The Bible tells us that God resists the proud. "Wherefore he saith, God resisteth the proud, but giveth grace unto the humble." (James 4:6). A proud person does not just have the devil to deal with, but God as well. Remember, if God is for you, no man can stand you; but if God is against you because of pride, I tell you, not even angels can help you. That was the predicament of Lucifer.

> **"Pride is a killer. It will kill your possibility of rising to higher heights in God. God cannot stand the sin of pride."**

How do you know when you or someone else you are dealing with is given to pride? How do usually know when pride is creeping in with regards to serving God?

What are the signs of pride? As we highlight these signs further, it will help you to honestly evaluate yourself to see if you are already a victim of pride.

Signs of Pride
1: Ascribing Results and Achievements to Yourself

When you begin to ascribe your results and achievements to yourself, you are already subscribing to pride. A good example of that is Nebuchadnezzar, king of Babylon. King Nebuchadnezzar was definitely a great king, with a massive and influential kingdom; but when he failed to realize that his greatness was only made possible by God Almighty, and fell into pride, he was destroyed.

> *The king spake, and said, is not this great Babylon, that*
> *I have built for the house of the kingdom by the might*
> *of my power, and for the honor of my majesty?*
>
> *Daniel 4:30.*

He was ascribing the greatness of Babylon to himself, and God became angry with him. His proud words from his prideful heart got him deeply in trouble with God. In fact, the words were still in his mouth when God declared a verdict against him.

> *While the word was in the king's mouth, there fell a*
> *voice from heaven, saying, O king Nebuchadnezzar, to*
> *thee it is spoken; The kingdom is departed from thee.*
> *And they shall drive thee from men, and thy dwelling*
> *shall be with the beasts of the field: they shall make*

thee eat grass as oxen, and seven times shall pass over
thee until thou know that the most high ruleth in the
kingdom of men, and giveth it to whomsoever he will.
The same hour was the thing fulfilled upon
Nebuchadnezzar: and he was driven from men, and
did eat grass as oxen, and his body was wet with the
dew of heaven, till his hairs were grown like eagles'
feathers, and his nails like birds' claws.

Daniel 4:31-33.

The reason is simple, he did not give God who gave him such opulent opportunity the glory. If you want to go far with God, and in life, never ascribe results and achievements to yourself. This is a very big temptation for a lot of people, but you will have to learn to always give God all the glory. I pray for you today; your blessings will not be taken away from you.

2: Oppressing People that are Below You in Any Way

When you begin to oppress people below you because now you are the director or boss at your office, you are walking in pride. If you are in the habit of oppressing your subordinates, it's a demonstration of pride. That is what Jesus referred to as "lording it over" people.

And he said unto them, the kings of the Gentiles
exercise lordship over them; and they that exercise
authority upon them are called benefactors. But ye shall
not be so: but he that is greatest among you, let him be
as the younger; and he that is chief, as he that doth
serve. Luke 22:25-26.

Pride makes you oppress people because they need favor from you or make access to you very difficult because God empowered you with a position where you can make decisions about people's promotion. Don't be like that. Be the kind of person that makes things easy for your subordinates.

3: Being Passive in the House of God or Watching People Serve While You Take the Back Seats to Be Served

Being passive in the house of God, and watching people serve while you sit and watch, is a major sign of pride in this regard. A prideful person doesn't want to get involved with others who are serving God in His house. They just sit back and feel distinguished while others clean the church, take care of the kids, or organize outreaches. However, Jesus made it clear that the greater person is not the one sitting down watching others serve, but the one who is willing to get his hands dirty serving others.

> **"***If you are in the habit of oppressing your subordinates, it's a demonstration of pride.***"**

4: Laying Too Much Importance on Yourself and Seeing Yourself Above Others

Attaching too much importance to yourself and seeing others as below you is a sign of pride. Pride will make you look down on your parents, spouse, neighbors, church members, or fellow workers at the office.

This is a very burdensome load to carry because you will only attract a demotion for yourself instead of a promotion. God cannot promote you if you perpetually look down on others. Besides, esteeming yourself beyond what you are really worth is self-deluding.

> *For if a man thinks himself to be something when he is nothing, he deceiveth himself. Galatians 6:3.*

However, if you know that you are a product of grace, you will learn to humble yourself, realizing that whatever you are and have, were given to you by the grace of God.

For who maketh thee to differ from another? and what
hast thou that thou didst not receive? now if thou didst
receive it, why dost thou glory, as if thou hadst not
received it? 1 Corinthian 4:7.

An Epitome of Humility

You can't really say for sure that you are humble until you have certain advantages in life. I am talking about such advantages that can sponsor your pride.

It is easy to be humble when you don't have anything, no money, no name, no fame, no obvious advantages. I know it is possible to be poor and very proud, but guess what, when you are really wealthy and powerful and yet humble, then that's real humility.

When you read about the humility of Jesus, you will have a clue to what I am talking about. Jesus was God in the flesh. He knew he was God. He had the power (still does), to heal the sick, raise the dead, and cast out the devil.

He had so much influence; because he was not the manger-man though He was manger-born. He was a very powerful influencer in His time, but He remained humble. In fact, it was that same humility that enabled him to lay aside the dignity of being God to become a man.

I love how the Bible describes that act of humility of His.

Let this mind be in you, which was also in Christ Jesus: Who, being in the form of God, thought it not robbery to be equal with God: But made himself of no reputation, and took upon him the form of a servant, and was made in the likeness of men: And being found in fashion as a man, he humbled himself, and became obedient unto death, even the death of the cross.

Philippians 2:5-8

Although He was God, He lived with such humility that anyone could easily miss Him for an ordinary man. Jesus was an epitome of humility. Jesus literally abandoned His glory and splendor in order to become a man. The Bible admonishes us to have such a mind — a mind that is so humble and obedient to the point of death. What does that tell us? Disobedience is a sign of pride.

"*If you are in the habit of oppressing your subordinates, it's a demonstration of pride.***"**

Notice: Jesus dropped all His reputation in order to be obedient to God. Humility involves dropping your reputation. The question is, have you dropped your own reputation? The internal turmoil you sometimes have towards obeying instructions is only a clear testament to the reputation you are yet to drop. Oh! yes! That's why many people get annoyed when you call their name without the titles they have or believe they have earned. This is so sad.

You need to understand that there is no real entitlement in titles, but there is divine lifting in humility. Amazingly, you cannot get it wrong, serving God with humility. Sometimes, it may seem like you are being used at the beginning, but I can assure you that if you continue to serve consistently and with humility, you will find yourself at the table of greatness.

I prophesy to you in the name of Jesus, you will not be demoted, and you will find rest and fulfillment at the top.

Service Motivated
by Love

Chapter Five
Service Motivated by Love

Your service to God must be powered by Love. In other words, love must be your primary source of motivation for service.

It doesn't matter if it's serving God in His house or serving humanity in terms of making your contribution in any sphere of society, love must be your main driving force. Otherwise, your motive is corrupted from day one, and your service will be totally unacceptable.

Never serve God because of what you need from Him. Serve God because you love Him. You must ensure that your motive is pure. A lot of people do things that are outrightly great by themselves, but because of impure motives, everything goes wrong eventually. This is one of the main reasons many businesses, relationships, and marriages do not work.

For example, some young ladies go into marriage because they discovered that the guy in question is wealthy. They decide to marry a man all because of what they think they can gain from him.

> **"Never serve God because of what you need from Him. Serve God because you love Him."**

They are not thinking about the character of the person perse; all they care about is the money. Unfortunately, that kind of relationship and marriage does not last. This is mainly due to impure motives, and selfishness driving the people. This does not necessarily have to do with ladies alone, but also with the men.

There are also some men who marry women for wrong motives. Maybe, there's something they need from that lady, or they have discovered that she has a good career, a good business, or they can see that she has money, and so they get into such marriages for such selfish reasons.

Now tell me, how can such a marriage succeed? They may start out enjoying themselves, but because it is built on the wrong precedence and foundation, sooner or later, the marriage will collapse. Remember, without the right foundation, a building has no future.

The Bible says,

> *"If the foundation be destroyed, what can the righteous do?" Psalm 11:3.*

That is exactly what happens when you see people that come to church, principally because they need something from God, or they want Him to meet their needs, as soon as they get what they want, they disappear. If they were looking and trusting God for a financial breakthrough, a job, or a spouse, the day they receive what they are looking for, they would be gone with the wind.

That is what I call transactional Christianity, which is the type of Christianity a lot of people have subscribed to these days. Do you know that some people join the church just because they need their Green Card or other forms of immigration settlement? Maybe, they are having problems with immigration and so on, and once they get what they came for, they just vanish. What they have done is that they have come to use God to meet their needs just like the relationship people have with commercial sex workers.

People who patronize commercial sex workers hardly

care how they fare; all they care about is satisfying their fleshly appetites. That is exactly how many people relate with God these days — with a motive that is outrightly selfish. Stop using God as though He prostitute.

What's Your Motivation?

There is a story told of the missionary, Hudson Taylor interviewing some youths who wanted to get involved with the work of missions. He asked them: "Why do you wish to become a foreign missionary?" One replied: "because Christ has commanded us to go into all the world and preach the Gospel to every creature." Another said: "because millions are dying without ever having heard of Jesus." Others gave similar answers, but not what Taylor sought. He replied:

> *"All of your motives are good, but I fear they will fail you in times of severe testing and tribulation — especially if you are confronted with the possibility of facing death for your testimony. The only motive that will enable you to remain true is stated in 2 Corinthians 5:14:*

> *"Christ's love constraining [compelling] you will keep you faithful in every situation."*

All through the scriptures, you will find different kinds of motivation for services to God. The book of Hebrews says:

Wherefore we receiving a kingdom which cannot be moved, let us have grace, whereby we may serve God acceptably with reverence and godly fear. Hebrews 12:28.

In other words, when you have an expectation of receiving kingdom benefits in eternity for your service to God, it will motivate you to serve God acceptably. In Paul's second letter to the Corinthians, he says that our service meets the needs of fellow believers *(2 Corinthians 9:12)*. If you know that what you are doing is adding value

to God's people and to the kingdom of God, then it would definitely motivate you to serve God. Also, there is a prospect of reward for all our labor of love. Nevertheless, though all these sources of motivation are powerful, but the truth is that love remains the greatest motivation for our work for God. As a matter of fact, it was love that motivated Christ's sacrificial work on the cross. In John's gospel, the Bible says God so loved the world that He gave His only begotten Son for our sake. His sacrifice was love motivated, and He expects us to serve Him motivated by love *(John 3:16)*.

When you try to imagine for once the reason Jesus Christ came to the earth in the first place, or why He would humble Himself so much that He literally became a man, you will see that it was a very challenging decision for Him. However, just like the apostle Paul, after contemplating this, concluded that this must be a mystery. He called it the mystery of godliness.

And without controversy great is the mystery of godliness:

God was manifest in the flesh, justified in the Spirit, seen of angels, preached unto the Gentiles, believed on in the world, received up into glory. 1 Timothy 3:16.

One thing is sure, it was pure unconditional love that motivated Jesus to come to us — humans and die for us to purchase our redemption.

"As a believer, you have the nature of God inside you and so, you have the capacity to love that way. You can love unconditionally like the gods."

The Greek word for such type of expression of unconditional love is the word, Agape. Agape can be defined first, as love like that of the gods. In fact, this kind of love is only possible with the gods. What this means is that ordinary mortals do not have the capacity to love in that dimension. Secondly, agape is an unconditional and sacrificial variant of love. It can be described as the sustained direction of the will for the good of another.

A person functioning in agape will take steps in direction and dimensions that are higher than that of ordinary mortals. As a believer, you have the nature of God inside you and so, you have the capacity to love that way.

You can love unconditionally like the gods. Why! Because you, being born again makes you an offspring of God, and because of that capacity in you, you are inspired and motivated to love God sacrificially and serve Him faithfully. In other words, love ought to be the principal motivation for everything we do, including our service to God.

The more we are aware of and experience God's love in our own lives, the more prone we are to respond in love by serving Him. Nobody can give what they don't have. So, unless we have first received this quality of love from Jesus Christ Himself, then we would be completely deficient in it; meaning we can't give it to other people. Our major reason for extending our lives towards God is only because He made the move first. God loved and served us when he sent Jesus to redeem us from sin.

Relationship is Key

Ultimately, our service to God naturally flows from our life of devotion to Him. The deeper we are devoted to God through fellowshipping with Him, the more we are disposed and willing to serve Him with every fiber of our being. As we fellowship with the Lord, we are continually brought into union with Him. As a result, we share in His desires and aspirations.

The more we fellowship with Him, the more we want to be and act like Him, realizing that it is in Him we live and move and have our being. So, an intimate relationship with the Lord is a major factor that influences us to not only serve Him but to serve others as well.

If you want to serve God, the key is to get to know Him! Ask the Holy Spirit to reveal more of God to you *(John 16:13)*. When we truly know God, who is love *(1 John 4:8)*, our natural response is a desire to love and serve Him in return. It has always been God's intention to make us like His Son, Jesus *(Romans 8:29)*.

When we look at Jesus' life, there's no denying that He was a servant. Jesus' entire life was centered on serving God — by teaching, healing, and proclaiming the Kingdom

(Matthew 4:23). He came not "to be served but to serve" *(Matthew 20:28).*

> **❝***The deeper we are devoted to God through fellowshipping with Him, the more we are disposed and willing to serve Him with every fiber of our being.***❞**

A Practical Example

As you read and study the scripture, you will find out that Jesus did not just come to die as our savior, but He also came to live as our example. Jesus is our perfect model of everything He taught while on earth.

One of the major virtues He practically modeled was service -I mean, serving with the right attitude. Do you remember how He washed the dirty feet of His disciples on the same night He was to be betrayed? Can you imagine how Jesus stooped so low to wash the feet of His disciples?

So, after he had washed their feet, and had taken his garments, and was set down again, he said unto them, know ye what I have done to you? Ye call me Master

In this was manifested the love of God toward us,
because that God sent his only begotten Son into the
world, that we might live through him. Herein is love,
not that we loved God, but that he loved us, and sent
his Son to be the propitiation for our sins. Beloved, if
God so loved us, we ought also to love one another. 1
John 4:9–11.

If you study the life of Apostle Paul, you will understand how an intimate relationship with God can go a long way in impacting our service to God. First, he was one of the chief persecutors of the church. In fact, before his supernatural encounter which resulted in his conversion, he had obtained permission from relevant authorities to go kill Christians in Damascus.

Nonetheless soon after encountering the Lord Jesus on his way, and the resulting relationship that ensued, he was recruited into kingdom service. However, prior to that, he had thought he was serving God, when in fact, he was an arch-enemy of God and His cause. Amazingly, after encountering Christ, he went on to be one of the most impactful Christian leaders of his day. Those who saw him after that were completely taken aback. The Bible says of him,

"And straightway he preached Christ in the

and Lord: and ye say well; for so I am. If I then, your Lord and Master, have washed your feet; ye also ought to wash one another's feet. For I have given you an example, that ye should do as I have done to you. Verily, verily, I say unto you, the servant is not greater than his lord; neither he that is sent greater than he that sent him. If ye know these things, happy are ye if ye do them. John 13:12–17.

All that was simply about modeling service as a lifestyle. Jesus wanted to demystify to His disciples the pride that usually goes with a high, exalted position in society. He wanted to show them how they could serve one another despite their status in life. Oh! my! he was a perfect example of service.

Genuine service cannot be separated from love. We can go through the motions of serving God, but if our hearts are not in it, we would be completely missing the point. According to the scriptures, it is very clear that, unless our service is rooted in love, it is outrightly meaningless *(1 Corinthians 13).* Generally, serving God out of a sense of obligation or duty, apart from love for God, is not what He desires. Rather, serving God should be our natural, love-filled response to Him who loved us first.

synagogues, that he is the Son of God." Acts 9:20.

From then on, he only grew in influence. As a matter of fact, his influence still lingers today through his epistles.

> **"** *We can go through the motions of serving God, but if our hearts are not in it, we would be completely missing the point.* **"**

In the book of Timothy, he expressed his gratitude to God, who delivered him from his former life into genuine service of God.

And I thank Christ Jesus for our Lord, who hath enabled me, for that he counted me faithful, putting me into the ministry, who was before a blasphemer, and a persecutor, and injurious: but I obtained mercy because I did it ignorantly in unbelief. And the grace of our Lord was exceeding abundant with faith and love which is in Christ Jesus. 1 Timothy 1:12–14.

This is so powerful because as soon as he became acquainted with the love and grace of God that is in Christ, his natural response was to serve God.

Unconditional Love

His love is not based on who you are, how you have behaved, what your income level is, what others think about you, or what promises you make in terms of reforming your life. He loves you because He loves you – no strings attached. You may be a person everyone knows and respects, or you may be a person nobody knows.

You could be a person who has never seen the inside of a jail or a person who has rarely seen the outside of one. Regardless, He says, "I love you." That's God for you. It is only those of us who know what it means to be loved unconditionally who can reach out to others with that same unconditional love. That kind of love is not just sacrificial, and unconditional, it is also compelling.

For the love of Christ constraineth us, because we thus judge, that if one died for all, then were all dead. 2 Corinthians 5:14.

Ultimately, love must be the foundation of acceptable service to God, or humanity. Amazingly, divine love requires sacrifice. Serving God requires serious sacrifice, so if you don't love Him enough, you will not have enough motivation to keep up with the many demands of service. To truly serve God, you have to serve Him as a seed.

A seed serves through its death. It is only through the death of the seed that it is able to produce *(John 12:24).*

As long as the seed is still alive, it cannot produce; but as soon as it surrenders to the soil and dies, it mass-produces itself.

> **"***It is only those of us who know what it means to be loved unconditionally who can reach out to others with that same unconditional love.***"**

It takes sacrifice to serve others with impact. I am reminded of the words of Ralph Waldo Emerson: *"It is one of the most powerful compensations of life that no man can sincerely try to help another without helping himself."* It was Albert Pine who said, "What we do for ourselves dies with us, but what we do for other people and the world is immortal." The question then is, what are you doing for other people or the world that will remain long after you are gone? It's up to you!

It is only those of us who know what it means to be loved unconditionally who can reach out to others with that same unconditional love.

Serving God is
Profitable

Chapter Six
Service Serving God is Profitable

Nothing on earth is as profitable and rewarding as serving God. Every acceptable service offered to God has rewards. You cannot serve God faithfully and go empty-handed.

One of the foremost revelations recommended in the scriptures, for anyone who would walk with God and serve Him, is that God is a rewarder. That knowledge is very powerful because once you get a hold of that fact, it automatically sets the tone for your walk and service to God, as well as humanity.

...for he that cometh to God must believe that he is and

that he is a rewarder of them that diligently seek him.

Hebrews 11:6.

If you don't know anything about God, at least, you should know that He exists and that HE IS A REWARDER.

> **"*Every acceptable service offered to God has rewards. You cannot serve God faithfully and go empty-handed.*"**

If you can't understand those two facts, forget it. In another scripture the scripture says, a child of God cannot seek God in vain:

> *I have not spoken in secret, in a dark place of the earth: I said not unto the seed of Jacob, seek ye me in vain: I the Lord speak righteousness, I declare things that are right. God has not asked us to seek him in vain, meaning that when we seek Him, He will not only be found but as we find Him and serve Him, we would definitely be rewarded. Isaiah 45:19.*

In essence, serving God is profitable. You cannot serve God and lose at the same time. The book of Job has this to say about our service to God:

> *If they obey and serve him, they shall spend their days in prosperity, and their years in pleasures. But if they*

obey not, they shall perish by the sword, and they shall
die without knowledge. Job 36:11.

God is a rewarder. In other words, your rewards are in the hands of God. If you are working in an organization, and you do your job with utmost commitment, excellence, and diligence, you are entitled to be rewarded financially, right? At the end of the work week or month, depending on what is obtainable in your nation, you expect a financial reward from your boss.

You cannot work for your boss at the office and expect your friend to pay your salary. In other words, your salary is the reward for your labor and input in your workplace.

In the same way, you cannot offer your service to God, and expect your reward from a man. Of course not! Instead, you need to look to God Almighty for your reward. If you are serving God in a church, for example, your reward is not in the hands of your pastor or any man but in the hands of God and God alone.

Failure to understand this fact is the reason many people who serve God get seriously frustrated and discouraged from their service to Him, especially when they have served God for a while.

The truth remains; that your reward is in the hands of God.

> *"Never be among those seeking the reward or even the applause of men. You cannot offer your service to God, and expect your reward from a man."*

This is why many people say that they served in a church and the pastor didn't come to say, "thank you." For them, they have served the pastor, and so he should find a way to reward them. I am not saying that people should not be appreciated for their service to a church, especially if they did whatever they did for the church in a volunteer capacity; but what I am saying is that if you begin to demand it, it shows that something was wrong with your heart and motive from the onset.

Never be among those seeking the reward or even the applause of men. The applause of men will not take you anywhere; but when God applauds and reward you, the rest will be history.

When you have served faithfully and acceptably, look to Jesus for your rewards.

In *Revelation 22:12;*

> *Jesus says behold, I come quickly; and my reward is with me, to give every man according as his work shall be.*

What Jesus is saying clearly is that He is the one who truly rewards, not your pastor, the poor, or any other person you served.

Settle It With God

These facts must be settled in your heart. As a pastor, and minister of God who served people by preaching, teaching, and praying for God's flock, I understand this very well. In fact, anytime I come for any church service for my ministerial duties, I always endeavor to settle it with God in prayer. I would usually pray and remind God that my rewards are with Him, and I can tell you, He has never disappointed me. Of course, there could be seasons of trials and things like that, which come and go, but I can assure you when it comes to rewards, God never fails. He always comes through for me.

God pays me well, and I mean, super well. I can tell you that serving Him is truly profitable. When you know for sure that God pays, it helps you to serve with the consciousness of an eminent divine reward. With that in place, you are able to serve God faithfully and consistently without murmuring or complaining.

Serving Others Is Serving God

The way to serve God is to serve other people. It is to strengthen the weak, enlighten the ignorant, empower the poor, and help those who cannot help themselves. Every time you assist someone who cannot help themselves, you are serving God.

The Bible says,

He that hath pity upon the poor lendeth unto the Lord,

and that which he hath given will he pay him again.

Proverbs 19:17.

Life is all about what you do for others. It is about how you use the resources at your disposal to make a positive difference in the lives of people. When you do that, you are indirectly serving God. In the words of human rights activist of blessed memory, Dr. Martin Luther King Jr., *"Life's most persistent and urgent question is what are you doing for others?"* Unfortunately, many people only care about themselves.

Nothing can be truer than the words of Dr. King. Claiming to serve God without serving men that are made in His image and likeness is self-delusion.

In Matthew's gospel, Jesus makes a clear connection between serving men and serving God. The illustration here is all about how God will reward those who serve their fellow men in His name.

> **"** *Life's most persistent and urgent question is what are you doing for others?" Unfortunately, many people only care about themselves.* **"**

When it was all said and done, the chief rewarder of men separated them for eternal rewards; not necessarily because of their service to God in church, but for how they served their fellow men:

> *When the Son of man shall come in his glory, and all the holy angels with him, then shall he sit upon the throne of his glory: And before him shall be gathered all nations: and he shall separate them one from another, as a shepherd divideth his sheep from the goats: And he shall set the sheep on his right hand, but the goats on the left. Then shall the King say unto them on his right hand, Come, ye blessed of my Father, inherit the kingdom prepared for you from the foundation of the world: For I was an hungered, and ye gave me meat:*

I was thirsty, and ye gave me drink: I was a stranger, and ye took me in: Naked, and ye clothed me: I was sick, and ye visited me: I was in prison, and ye came unto me. Then shall the righteous answer him, saying, Lord, when saw we thee an hungered and fed thee? or thirsty, and gave thee drink? When saw we thee a stranger, and took thee in? or naked, and clothed thee? Or when saw we thee sick, or in prison, and came unto thee? And the King shall answer and say unto them, Verily I say unto you, inasmuch as ye have done it unto one of the least of these my brethren, ye have done it unto me. Matthew 25:31-40.

Actually, for a lot of people (believers), this is where we are falling short. For many people, life is all about them. They live as though the earth revolves around their orbit. Their lives clearly exemplify what someone rightly termed, "me, myself and I syndrome." Of course, we know we are in the last days and one of the scripturally acknowledged characteristics of the last days is that men will be lovers of themselves, and selfish.

This know also, that in the last days perilous times shall come. For men shall be lovers of their own selves, covetous, boasters, proud, blasphemers...
2 Timothy 3:1-2.

While this may be unacceptably so among non-believers in Christ, it must not be so for us. We must learn how to be selfless, and outward-focused with the intent that we may use whatever we are and have to make a difference in our world.

For some people, this has become so bad that they would even go as far as making very critical life-uttering decisions without the consent of their spouse. Imagine a lady who goes to abort her unborn baby without the consent of her husband. That is pure selfishness. As much as such an act is despicable, it is even worse because of the fact that it was done solely; I mean, without the consent of people who matter to her. How can a person decide without even giving a second thought as to how their decision or choice will affect their families and friends?

Why don't people think about the ripple effect that their decisions can have on their entire household before making those decisions? That is the way selfishness works in the life of those who are selfish. Little wonder such people believe and behave like everybody owes them and must give to them, yet they cannot give to another person. This is a very sad situation, but it is true!

As a believer in Christ, you cannot be that way. You must exchange selfishness for selflessness, stinginess for generosity, and a desire to lord over people for a passion to serve others genuinely. However, in order for you to serve God the way you ought to, you need to thoroughly understand the benefits of serving God.

Benefits Of Serving God

There are numerous benefits accrued to serving God, some of these are highlighted below.

1: Service Distinguishes You from Your Peers and Colleagues

If you are one of those thinking that serving God is a waste of time, please think again. You know, one time, God's people thought it was unprofitable to serve God, and questioned their commitment to God.

In other words, they were saying among themselves, "we have been serving God all along, what have we gained? Of what profit is serving God? They were really discouraged by life's challenging experiences that they questioned their commitment.

In fact, they had wondered why wicked people who didn't serve God seemed to thrive. It was so bad that God had to send His prophets to enlighten and encourage them to continue in their service to God.

Ye have said, it is vain to serve God: and what profit is it that we have kept his ordinance, and that we have

walked mournfully before the Lord of hosts? And now
we call the proud happy; yea, they that work
wickedness are set up; yea, they that tempt God are
even delivered. Then they that feared the Lord spake
often one to another: and the Lord hearkened, and
heard it, and a book of remembrance was written
before him for them that feared the Lord, and that
thought upon his name. And they shall be mine, saith
the Lord of hosts, in that day when I make up my
jewels; and I will spare them, as a man spareth his own
son that serveth him. Then shall ye return, and discern
between the righteous and the wicked, between him
that serveth God and him that serveth him not.
Malachi 3:14-18.

One of the lessons from the above scripture is that God has a book of remembrance where all your service, and like the Bible calls it, your labor of love is recorded. Therefore, because they are recorded, they can be recalled and, of course, rewarded. That means the rewards of our service are guaranteed by God. Secondly, it says that God will distinguish between those who serve Him from those who don't.

God promised to make the difference so clear and nonambiguous that no one will be able to confuse those who serve God for those who do not serve Him. God was talking about a certain type of separation that will set His servants apart from others. Sincerely, if you understand this, you will never be discouraged another day in your life. I pray for you that none of your colleagues, your mates, or your peers will be able to match up with you. None of your contemporaries will be able to rise above you in the name of Jesus.

2: Service Qualifies You for Unending Greatness

In the kingdom of God, we play by a direct set of rules. The people of the world can become great simply by exerting themselves on other people, however, in the kingdom of God, service is the password to the place of greatness. If you master service, you have mastered greatness. When you choose to subscribe to a life of service, you have automatically subscribed to unending greatness.

But he that is greatest among you shall be your servant.

And whosoever shall exalt himself shall be abased, and

he that shall humble himself shall be exalted.

Matthew 23:11,12.

The more you serve, the greater you become. Amazingly, this cuts across different fields of life, career, and business. In the business world, the more you sell to your clients, the greater you will rise.

> **"When you choose to subscribe to a life of service, you have automatically subscribed to unending greatness."**

As long as your products and services are good, and solve problems for a significant number of people, then you are just on your way to greatness. It holds that the more you serve people, the more referrals you will get.

3: When You Serve God, You Are Exempted from Calamity

When you serve God, you become His kingdom diplomat, and as a kingdom diplomat, you are entitled to diplomatic immunity. As a person who is given to the service of God, you are exempted from calamity. When the wave of destruction and calamity shows up in a place, it may affect every other person but not those who are confirmed servants of the most high God.

In the book of Malachi, he used the word 'spare' to tell us about His commitment to exempt His servants from evil, calamity, and misfortunes.

"...and I will spare them, as a man spareth his own son

that serveth him." Malachi 3:17.

You cannot serve the Almighty God and your protection and safety will not be guaranteed; it's not possible. God is too responsible to abandon His own when they need Him the most, and that is why the Bible says, no weapon fashioned against you shall prosper. However, the Bible makes it very clear to us that this declaration is particularly reserved for servants of God (not for just anybody).

> *No weapon that is formed against thee shall prosper, and every tongue that shall rise against thee in judgment thou shalt condemn. This is the heritage of the servants of the Lord, and their righteousness is of me, saith the Lord. Isaiah 54:17.*

God did not promise you and I that there would be no attempt against us, He did not promise a hitch-free ride through life; what He definitely promised is that whatever they fashion against you will not prosper. No evil will succeed against you, as a servant of God. That is His exemption program at work. Part of how He does it is to bless your bread and your water and take sickness away from your house **(Exodus 23:25).** When your bread and water are blessed, sicknesses will naturally stay away from you because our bread and water constitute a major source of good health.

> **❝** *When the wave of destruction and calamity shows up in a place, it may affect every other person but not those who are confirmed servants of the most high God.* **❞**

4: Serving God Brings You into Active Partnership with God

When you are serving God, you are partnering with Him to bring His purpose to pass on the earth. In 1 Corinthians 3:9; the Bible says, "...we are Laborers together with God..." Everyone serving God is in God's business.

The truth is that many people live off God, but only a few people labor with God. In an organization, who gets paid more between the worker and the partner?

The partner, of course! A partner brings more to the table than a mere staff or employee, as a result, he benefits more. You cannot take out of an organization or a system more than the proportion of input you make into it. Usually, a worker is paid according to his work per hour, but the partner is paid based on the percentage of profit agreed upon. What's the difference between the partner and the worker? A partner thinks of what he will add to the business, not just what he will take, but the focus of a worker or employee is on how much salary he or she will take away at the end of the work week. Stop being a mere worker for God, become a co-laborer with Him.

5: When You Serve God, God Himself Exalts and Promotes You

Promotion is a word reserved for those who serve faithfully. You don't promote an idle or unproductive person.

Your job is to serve God, His responsibility is to promote you. Remember, promotion comes only from God. If your promotion comes from a man, I tell you what, it won't last at all. In fact, you will need your strength to sustain it, but when God Almighty promotes you, it is permanent.

That means, nobody will be able to take it away from you. Jesus, though the son of God, surrendered Himself in the service of God, I mean, literally serving God's agenda to the point of paying the ultimate price — death on the cross. However, the good news remains, that God, exalted Him above anything you can think of *(Philippines 2:8-9)*.

That is the way it works with God. You cannot serve God and not enjoy the many benefits that go with it. It's not possible! I pray that as you will imbibe the culture of service to God and man, God almighty will crown your effort with greatness.

Empowered to Serve

Chapter Seven

Empowered to Serve

E very believer is saved to serve. In other words, the main reason you escaped from sin, Satan, and the world is for you to serve God.

This is a fact that we have already established in a preceding chapter. However, faithfulness is a major requirement for anyone who seeks to serve God.

As believers, we must serve God faithfully and consistently. Without faithfulness in our service to God, there will be no reward. God does not measure the size of your service as much as He does your faithfulness.

We have to be faithful in service. The book of Proverbs talks about faithfulness, Most men will proclaim every one his own goodness:

> *but a faithful man who can find? Proverbs 20:6.*

What the scripture above means is that faithfulness is not an easy quality to come by. However, for believers, it should not be so, because we are born again with the fruit of faithfulness. In other words, we have the capacity to be faithful. More so, as a child of God, you are a minister, and as such, you are expected to discharge your duties of service faithfully.

That is exactly what Apostle Paul said in his second letter to the Corinthian church:

> *Let a man so account of us, as of the ministers of Christ,*
> *and stewards of the mysteries of God. Moreover, it is*
> *required in stewards, that a man be found faithful. 2*
> *Corinthians 2:4.*

It is pertinent to say however that in order to serve God faithfully and reap the many rewards of service, we must understand the place of empowerment. Majority of the time, God's demands of us are way beyond what we can accomplish by ourselves. More so, God derives glory from seeing us depend on Him to do His will and accomplish His assignments and purpose for our lives.

Consequently, we need divine empowerment. Secondly,

we have to realize that anything that is of God will be readily resisted by Satan and his kingdom. In other words, without empowerment from God, we would fall flat before satanic resistance and attacks. However, with supernatural empowerment, which is available to every believer in Christ, the devil is no match. It takes divine power to subdue the devil and his many activities.

Say unto God, how terrible art thou in thy works!
through the greatness of thy power shall thine enemies
submit themselves unto thee. Psalm 66:3.

The devil can contend with philosophy, he can be content with your good intentions and your well-packaged programs, but he cannot contend with the divine power of God. This is especially so when you truly surrender yourself to serve God with the whole of your being —in complete obedience to His will.
That is why the Bible says,

"Submit yourselves therefore to God. Resist the devil,
and he will flee from you." James 4:7.

On the other hand, a human being at his best is still human, laden with all kinds of inadequacies, weaknesses, limitations, and inconsistencies. Without empowerment, you can't really do much for God or for your world. Divine empowerment is, therefore, imperative for effective service.

For instance, before the disciples of Jesus could effectively dispense the gospel, they were divinely empowered. While Jesus knew He would commit the preaching of the gospel to His disciples, He also knew that they could not do it without empowerment, even though they had spent three and a half years of thorough training with the chief shepherded Himself.

> **"*Without empowerment, you can't really do much for God or for your world. Divine empowerment is, therefore, imperative for effective service.*"**

Jesus, the son of the Almighty God knew that without empowerment, His disciples were going to fail flat, and come short of God's intention and assignment for their lives. So, He said they should wait to be empowered to serve God effectively.

> *And, behold, I send the promise of my Father upon you: but tarry ye in the city of Jerusalem, until ye be endued with power from on high.*
> *Luke 24:49.*

Divine empowerment is the precursor for the effective fulfillment of any divine assignment. Without it, forget about fulfilling your assignment to the glory of God.

Why You Need Empowerment

Here are a few very important reasons why you need empowerment for service.

1. Your Flesh is Always at War Against Your Spirit

One of the major reasons you need to be empowered by God is due to the weakness of the flesh. Although you are a spirit, you live in the body, and because of that, you are subject to various limitations. In other words, being humans, we are more drawn to physical and sensual desires than spiritual things. The flesh prefers to do things that are convenient to the natural man, things that come easy with his soul life.

This is a lesson that the disciples of Jesus would later learn the hard way. It was a few hours before the betrayal and crucifixion of Jesus, and He took His disciples to the mountain to pray. Of course, He expected them to pray alongside him.

Unfortunately, these disciples were busy sleeping most of the time. Sure, they were not sleeping because they wanted to sleep, and abandon their spiritual responsibilities; but they couldn't help it.

They only yielded to the call of nature. I am pretty sure they must have put up a fight against sleep, yet sleep overpowered them. Having been busy working and doing ministry with Jesus; they were exhausted from much engagement. In essence, their sleep could be justified in the sense that they had been busy with work. Yet, it was a major mistake to have allowed sleep to rob them of such a destiny moment.

> **"*The flesh prefers to do things that are convenient to the natural man, things that come easy with his soul life.*"**

Although Jesus tried once and again to awaken them to pray alongside Him, they were too tired to stay awake let alone pray, and that was why Jesus gave them an amazing spiritual lecture:

> *Then saith he unto them, my soul is exceeding sorrowful, even unto death: tarry ye here, and watch with me. And he went a little further, and fell on his face, and prayed, saying, O my Father,*

if it is possible, let this cup pass from me: nevertheless, not as I will but as thou wilt. And he cometh unto the disciples, and findeth them asleep, and saith unto Peter, what, could ye not watch with me, one hour? Watch and pray, that ye enter not into temptation: the spirit indeed is willing, but the flesh is weak. Matthew 26:38-42.

There is no doubt that the spirit is willing, but the willingness of the spirit does not guarantee the performance of the flesh. Of course not! We are told that the flesh is weak. The spirit wants to pray, but the flesh wants to sleep. The spirit wants to forgive, but the flesh wants to hold onto a grudge, be bitter, or live in malice. The spirit wants to give, but the flesh wants to hold back everything to itself. The flesh has no generosity, but selfishness.

That is exactly how it works with every other area; the spirits' desire runs in the opposite direction from the desires of your flesh, and the ultimate result is a struggle to do what is expected of you. In fact, most times, failure, and disappointment are the end result of such opposition between the spirit and the flesh. However, the more you yield to the desires of the spirit, the more the spirit gains take actions and initiatives that will bring glory to God. The devil is very much aware of the devastating impact of the spirit of discouragement on the life of a believer. That is why he will stop at nothing to resist you and stop you from making progress and succeeding at what you do. According to the Britannica Dictionary, "discouragement is the act of making something less likely to happen or of making people less likely to do something that they intend to do. It is a feeling of having lost hope or confidence. Discouragement also refers to something (such as a failure or difficulty) that discourages someone."

When people fail to succeed in their endeavors or lack the resources to carry out their purposes, discouragement sets in. That's the truth. Discouragements will come, and if you don't know how to handle them, you will be completely knocked out.

You must learn to handle discouragement as a child of God. A good example of someone who went through discouragement in the scriptures is David. David and his men experienced a major setback on the battlefield. The Philistine army invaded Ziklag, David's base, and took the spoils of his wives and those of his men. When David and his men returned and found out what had happened in their absence, everybody was deeply discouraged.

The Bible says that they were greatly distressed. It was a

ascendancy over the flesh. Otherwise, the flesh will continue to dominate. For this reason, you need the supernatural empowerment of God to enable you to do things that do not come naturally to you. Service doesn't come naturally, so you need empowerment to serve.

Your flesh will always give you reasons why you cannot serve. I am not gifted, they will gossip about me, all eyes will be on me, and so on are all some excuses the flesh tries to use to stop you from serving God. However, as you decide to serve God and are empowered by Him, all those self-imposed limitations will gradually leave your life.

> **"***The willingness of the spirit does not guarantee the performance of the flesh.***"**

2. You Need Empowerment So You Can Be Constantly Encouraged in the Lord

During the period of your various services to God, there would be heavy discouragements. The truth is that discouragement is one of the greatest weapons of the devil to sway many believers away from a life of faithful service to God.

When you are discouraged, you will lack the motivation to

really bad situation for him and all of his army. It was so bad that his own men were contemplating stoning him. Imagine, the same people he had fought for and labored with all along, the same people he had trained over the years intending to stone him. It was that bad, but thank God, David eventually encouraged himself in the Lord.

And David was greatly distressed; for the people spake of stoning him, because the soul of all the people was grieved, every man for his sons and for his daughters: but David encouraged himself in the Lord his God. 1 Samuel 30:6.

Of course, after he had encouraged himself, he enquired from God whether or not he should attack, and God's response was in the affirmative.

Long story short, David and his men pursued after the Philistines, and with the help of God, they were able to recover everything and everyone that was taken captive and returned with many spoils. Do you know that, if David had not encouraged himself in the Lord, he wouldn't have had the capacity to pursue after them to the extent of recovering all that was earlier lost?

Never allow discouragement to thrive around you. By the way, discouragement is inevitable. As long as you are alive and actively engaged in the pursuit of your purpose in God, you will face discouragement.

Things will discourage you; people will discourage you, and the demands of your commitments to your local church will sometimes inconvenience and discourage you, but you must refuse to be discouraged. Just like the Bible says of David, you must learn how to encourage yourself in the Lord. Decide to live above every discouragement. It is a personal decision. In other words, it's totally up to you. Nobody will do it for you.

3. You Need Empowerment for Service So You Can Focus Your Eyes on Whom You Are Serving

When you are truly empowered by God for service, your focus will be on God Himself. It is a tragedy to put your focus on a man while serving the almighty God. The worst category is the set of people who think they are serving the church or the pastor. If you are like that, obviously, you cannot serve God faithfully and consistently. You must fix your gaze on Jesus. Remember, Jesus is the author and finisher of your faith.

Wherefore seeing we also are compassed about with so great a cloud of witnesses, let us lay aside every weight, and the sin which doth so easily

beset us, and let us run with patience the race
that is set before us, looking unto Jesus the author
and finisher of our faith; who for the joy that
was set before him endured the cross, despising
the shame and is set down at the right hand of the
throne of God. Hebrews 12:1-2.

When you look onto Jesus, you can endure anything that comes in between you and your service to God. It doesn't matter how much you gossip about a person whose focus is on Jesus, they are not moved because their focus is where it should be, on God. People whose focus is not entirely on God are easily offended when a challenge comes up regarding their service to Him.

4: You Need Empowerment to Serve with the Right Heart Which Will Cause God to Reward You in Due Season

Empowerment enables you to serve God with the right heart, and quite frankly, there is absolutely no substitute for serving God with the right heart.

A lot of people are serving God, the problem is that it's not with the right heart, attitude, and motive. We have already done justice to the subject of seeking with the right heart in a previous chapter, but I still want to emphasize it because of the pivotal role it plays. To serve God with the right heart, you need to do it by Faith. Hebrews 11:6; says, ...without faith it is impossible to please him: for he that cometh to God must believe that he is and that he is a rewarder of them that diligently seek him.

❝*Decide to live above every discouragement. It is a personal decision.***❞**

We also looked at the fact that serving God is highly profitable, but it takes Faith to serve Him with the right heart to enjoy those benefits. When you are empowered, the power of God helps you to fix your heart on the right motive of serving God to please Him. Just like we have seen, it must be done by faith.

5: You Need Empowerment So You Can Serve God till the End of Your Days

You need empowerment to sustain your service. The Bible talks about serving God with fervency.

"Not slothful in business; fervent in spirit; serving the Lord; Rejoicing in hope; patient in tribulation; continuing instant in prayer." Romans 12:11.

To be fervent in the spirit of serving the Lord requires the

As a young pastor in a ministry called Living Faith Church Worldwide (also known as Winners Chapel), I was deployed to a particular place to go and serve there.

That was the place where Bishop David Oyedepo's (who is the presiding bishop) Mum worshipped. At that time, she was still alive and was about 85 years old or thereabout. Do you know that that old woman who should be resting and enjoying her labor would still be the one to clean the church?

She will sweep a portion of the church, and sit down a little to regain her strength, and sometimes, we would try to stop her, but she will refuse. She would tell you in the Yoruba language, "my son, I can't stop serving now, this is what brought me to where I am today." Every time she talked like this; my heart would melt.

Do you know what made the difference? She was working with a revelation; she knew exactly what she was doing and what to expect from it. She was never looking for any man to notice, applaud, or reward her for what she did in the kingdom of her father. She knew it is a great privilege to serve God, and for that privilege, we were eternally thankful to God.

Let's stop trying to jump from the floor to the top, let's start using the legitimate route and path to greatness —

empowerment that comes from God as the scripture above says. Notice further, that there is a connection between fervency in the spirit and serving God.

It says additionally that when you are fervent, you are able to continue patiently in tribulation, and in prayer. Meaning that you can stand in difficult seasons of your service to God. That is the place of empowerment. A lot of folks start out seeking and serving God with a blazing passion, but sooner or later they begin to faint.

Without divine empowerment, you may start serving God, but somewhere along the line, when challenges show up, you are easily knocked out, and you fall by the wayside. Starting is very important but starting holds no value unless you are ready to persist until the end.

Not everyone who started well with God finished well with Him, and that is the reason you have to strive very hard to get to the end in order to be rewarded. Remember, he that endures to the end is the one that shall be saved. You need empowerment to remain in service until the end.

Serve With Understanding

To serve God effectively, you need a revelation of what you are doing. I saw something very humbling years ago.

which is service, both to God and man. It may seem slow but stay with it, and serve your way to the topmost top, and to greatness. Don't be like those who live by cutting corners, instead be like the great examples of men and women all through history who through selfless service and hard work were able to attain the place of greatness.

Remember, the secret of men is in their stories, and as you begin to seek after the wisdom of these select few, you will be well on your own path to greatness in your generation. Just like the scripture rightly says about David that "...after he had served his own generation by the will of God, fell on sleep, and was laid unto his fathers, and saw no corruption." *I pray passionately for you that you will not see corruption until you have served your own generation and those coming after you (if Jesus tarries).*

May you not only find that solemn path of greatness but may you walk the path of greatness. May you become a testament to the principle and power of serving God faithfully and with humility. May you serve Him to the end, and may you be rewarded with estates both in time and eternity! Receive that grace in Jesus' name!

OTHER BOOKS BY AUTHOR

GO HIGHER: TAKE YOUR LIFE TO THE NEXT LEVEL

Going higher is tough, and can sometimes be extremely hard. I don't think anyone would argue with that fact. As cool and desirable as changing of status might seem, it comes with a lot of responsibilities, born from the womb of intention.

It's not about being ambitious, you just know deep within you that this is no more your level.

Going higher is as natural as an eagle soaring effortlessly up there, while other birds struggle to attain those beautiful heights. Unfortunately, quite a good number of us live below our God-ordained status. We remain at the same level for such a long time, that we become like a river that is not flowing anymore, hence, start losing color, freshness, beauty, purpose for creation, and starts stinking so bad.

Without any doubt, we are convinced that we are made for more, we have outgrown our present space and sphere, but ignorance, fear, and sometimes forces beyond us pin us down to the same spot, whilst we maintain the status quo. We see people and entities far and near go higher because they chose to make those daring moves.

Until there is an inner reaction, there might never be corresponding actions that will birth the change we desire. The good news is that what you need to take that first leap is already in you. All you need is to realize that the low places are crowded and the topmost top where your Creator resides is calling your name each moment, telling you to come a bit higher.

In case what you've read above sounds a bit true, why wait further? Now is the time to wake up, get up, stand up, look around you, react against your present level, and GO HIGHER!

WHEN MONEY FAILS

In this masterpiece, Olumayowa Oke analyzes some pertinent matters that will expand your understanding of the value of money as different things to different people. The book further dissects issues such as:

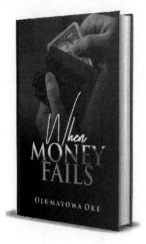

→ Understanding Biblical Prophecies
→ From Revelation to Fulfillment
→ Can you pray biblical prophecies away or avert them?
→ End Time Prophecies and Digital Currency
→ How to embrace and maximize the new order of things
→ Positioning yourself for the unexpected shift in wealth
→ Pursuing the Anointing of the Sons of Issachar, which is understanding the times and seasons we are in
→ How to engage the weapon of prayer to shift things
→ Strategies to enjoy surplus in scarcity

THE PLAGUE CALLED RACISM

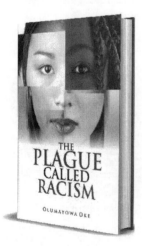

In this Amazing Book, you will discover the following keys, among others:

→ Why people are racists
→ How to reduce racism against blacks
→ The power of synergy
→ Economic Empowerment for blacks
→ Why you should get involved with politics
→ Eliminate inferiority complex
→ Power to break racial barriers

Faith That Conquers

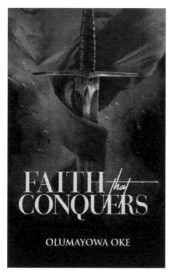

Greater Faith is an uncommon and an ever winning supernatural force that enables any human being to dominate and subdue the challenges of life. Greater Faith will surmount any mountain any day, any time, regardless of how high the mountain is.

Every good thing in my life as an individual today has no root from me, because they can all be traced to the finger of God at work. You must be aware that the easiest way to move the finger of God is through your active faith. It is this same level of active faith that I am trusting God to impart to you via this book.

Greater Faith is the answer to all simply because God can do nothing without your faith. Faith is the unchangeable currency of heaven through which transactions are made.

Revive Us Again

Although, revival and spiritual awakening are the Lord's work, yet meeting the conditions of revival is the work of man. There is a God part as well as the human part in any revival.

Revival is not a sovereign act of God that occurs without man's impute, no. Although it is initiated by God, it is not automatic. In other words, you don't just passively wait for revival, rather, you can pay the price to make revival happen.

God is a God of purpose, plans, and objectivity. He is also a God of patterns. He told Moses to ensure he build the tabernacle according to the pattern He showed him on the mount (Exo. 25:40).

Made in the USA
Middletown, DE
02 November 2022

13881054R00080